THE OTHER RED LINE

WASHINGTON STREET, FROM SCOLLAY SQUARE TO THE COMBAT ZONE

ANTHONY M. SAMMARCO

AMERICA
THROUGH TIME®
ADDING COLOR TO AMERICAN HISTORY

This book is dedicated to Bradley Jay,
the popular host of "Jay Talking" on WBZ Radio 1030
iHeartRadio who suggested the topic of this book,
and also to his wonderful listening family

America Through Time is an imprint of Fonthill Media LLC
www.through-time.com
office@through-time.com

Published by Arcadia Publishing by arrangement with Fonthill Media LLC
For all general information, please contact Arcadia Publishing:
Telephone: 843-853-2070
Fax: 843-853-0044
E-mail: sales@arcadiapublishing.com
For customer service and orders:
Toll-Free 1-888-313-2665

www.arcadiapublishing.com

First published 2021

ISBN 978-1-63499-333-3

Typeset in Mrs Eaves XL Serif Narrow
Printed and bound in England

CONTENTS

Acknowledgments

Joel Andreasen; Jessica Berson; Boston Public Library, David Leonard; Howie Carr, *Boston Herald*; Hutchinson and Pasqualina Cedmarco; Cesidio "Joe" Cedrone; the late Frank Cheney; Edie Clifford; Peter Coccaro; Colortek, Jackie Anderson; The Croce Collection, Elaine Croce; eBay; Danny Goldsmith; Edward Gordon; Katherine Greenough; Joann Gricus; Helen Hannon; Bradley Jay, "Jay Talking" WBZ 1030/iHeart Radio; George Kalchev, Fonthill Media; Peter B. Kingman; David Kruh, author of *Scollay Square* and *Always Something Doing*; Lauren Leja; Dr. George Letsou; John E. Lynes; Kenneth McIntyre; Massachusetts Institute of Technology, Rotch Visual Collections; Eddie Mulkern; Museum of Fine Arts, Boston; the late Robert Neiley, AIA; Orleans Camera; the late Roger Prouty; The Red Hat; Jeff Rubin; Jodi Rudoren, editor *The Forward*; Anthony Salvucci, for a piece of "Scollay Square Under;" Ron Scully; Robert Bayard Severy; Maureen Smith; Robert W. Stone; Alan Sutton, Fonthill Media; Kenneth Turino and Chris Matthias; University of Massachusetts, Archives and Special Collections, Sammarco Collection.

Washington Street, for all of its historic and mercantile aspects, was to also include from the late 1950s to the 1990s the infamous Combat Zone, an area of the city that was on one hand dangerous and on the other titillating. As this sign so poignantly states: "You have nothing to fear except fear itself!" So, welcome to the *Other Red Line*.

INTRODUCTION

Burlesque as you like it—The Poor man's Follies!

Washington Street in Boston was named in 1788 in honor of George Washington, the first president of the United States. The street, which is the longest in Massachusetts, was originally known by four different names in the eighteenth century, from Kneeland Street to Court Street, less than a mile in length, and was known as Orange Street, Newbury Street, Marlborough Street, and Cornhill, even though it was a contiguous thoroughfare.

In the decade after Boston embraced a municipal form of government in 1822, the city began to change both topographically as well as through matriculation and immigration. After Beacon Hill had been leveled in the early nineteenth century, with fill used to create the Flat of Beacon Hill, the same was undertaken on Pemberton Hill, one of the three hills of Boston in the 1830s. Developed as one of the two squares on Beacon Hill with red brick row houses facing a center park, Pemberton Square attracted many affluent families in Boston, some with China Trade connections. At the foot of the hill, a row of red brick commercial buildings were built along Court Street facing Scollay Square, the transportation of the city which was named in 1838 after William Scollay. The new neighborhood was the epitome of urbane elegance and would remain as such until just before the Civil War. As commercial development began to encroach, many of the row houses became schools, offices, and the police headquarters, and the Adventist Millerite Temple on Howard Street became the Howard Athenaeum, where it was said to host popular performances of "opera, tragedy, comedy, burlesque, vaudeville, minstrels, and magicians." As Boston's demographics changed, so too did the neighborhood, and by 1870, Scollay Square had become a destination, partly because of its places of entertainment but also because of its ease of accessibility, as the horse-drawn streetcars linked it to other parts of the city, the suburbs and surrounding cities and towns.

The result was that the Howard Athenaeum, which featured musicals and traveling theatrical groups, began to show burlesque and comedy acts that attracted people of all ages, and in 1869, it introduced an era of bawdy vaudeville acts with "Lydia Thompson and Her British Blondes." As Thomas H. O'Connor said: "Scollay Square [had] become a place where tattoo parlors, barrooms, shooting galleries, photography studios, shabby movie theaters, gaudy hot dog stands, and sleazy burlesque houses blighted what had once been a quiet residential district." With burlesque houses such as the Old Howard, which dropped "Athenaeum" from its name in 1898, and the Crawford House, movie palaces began to open, showing silent films accompanied by a pianist, news reels and comedy acts. The New Palace Theatre, the Star Theatre, the Theatre Comique, and the Scollay Square Olympia offered vaudeville as well as silent films, which were a novelty at the time. With so many people seeking entertainment in Scollay Square, restaurants, bars, and sandwich shops offered an entertaining evening out. Scollay Square quickly became a bustling array of nightclubs packed with soldiers and sailors, politicians, businessmen, couples on dates, and the single man seeking a night of fun. However, there were also censors and the ever-watchful eye of the Boston Watch and Ward Society, perpetually on guard for indecency, but perhaps willing to look the other way if the price was right. As David Kruh said: "By 1910, the evolution of Scollay Square was complete. The Old Howard was pure burlesque, and every sailor who got liberty in Boston was making it a point to visit the Square. What the Brahmins and the Yankees had abandoned, others were quick to make their own."

Burlesque was now king, and the anointed queens of burlesque danced at both the Crawford House and the Old Howard, as well as smaller clubs, which were renowned, not just in Boston, but incredibly even around the world, and had well-known performers who were beloved by their audience. It was not just adult men who typically patronized the burlesque theaters, but as Alison Arnold of the *Boston Globe* so sardonically said: "Many a Harvard freshman sneaked into the Old Howard and glanced furtively around to see if there was anyone who would recognize him and tell his old man he'd been there. As he was going out, one young man was chagrined to meet his father going in!" During World War II, Scollay Square had literally become a vortex that seemed to draw people of all walks of life to the unabated excitement of the nightly entertainment that left no one the same as when they arrived. Unfortunately, nothing can remain the same, and with the ever present city censor and the vigilant New England Watch and Ward Society, the burlesque stars saw their acts scrutinized, which was to abruptly come to an end when the Old Howard was closed in 1953 with multiple charges of indecency. People from all walks of life petitioned John B. Hynes, the mayor of Boston, for it to be reopened, which alas was a furtive attempt and Francis W. Hatch sarcastically said it in his lament "Sailor's Haven."

Some coward closed the Old Howard
We don't have Burley anymore!

Scollay Square came to an end in 1962, when the Old Howard Casino Theatre on Hanover Street was razed. Unfortunately, many Proper Bostonians were said to have breathed a sigh of relief with the demise of what was often referred to as the local den of iniquity and welcomed the proposed development of Government Center; however, an iconic and well-beloved entertainment district was obliterated in the name of urban renewal.

However, Washington Street, that age-old thoroughfare, was not only a place of department stores, specialty shops, restaurants, and theaters, but also the link from Scollay Square to the Combat Zone, which paralleled the Red Line of the MBTA. The area of Washington Street, between Kneeland and Boylston Street, was developed in the late nineteenth century with low rise buildings with ground-floor shops and offices and small businesses above as well as impressive theaters that rivaled those in Scollay Square. Among them were the Gaiety Theatre, the State Theatre, the Paramount Theatre, the Mayflower Theatre, and the Globe Theatre, all of which offered entertainment, initially with burlesque but more increasingly with silent films, and were posh theaters that vied for patrons and would attract them with sumptuous interiors, comfortable seating, and orchestras that played in the lobby. The area was vibrant and first run films were often shown, but as Scollay Square's luster began to tarnish, even before it was swept away by the urban renewal of the early 1960s, Washington Street south of Avery Street began to see an increasing change in the character of the neighborhood. With bars, strip clubs, and theaters beginning to show adult X-rated movies, the area increasingly became a place that one either went out of his way to avoid, or found so alluring that the inevitability of joining in the irreverent fun of it all quickly overcame one's reservations. The new name of the neighborhood was the "Combat Zone," which was coined when in 1951 Judge George Roberts said of the area that "It is really a Combat Zone." It was also popularized through a series of exposé articles on the area by Jean Cole, a writer for the *Boston Daily Record* in the 1960s. In the 1970s, there were over thirty sex-related businesses, including adult bookstores, peep shows, and nude dancing venues along lower Washington Street. The Combat Zone was spiraling uncontrollably as a world unto itself, at once sordid and the other titillating. Sam Allis, a writer at the *Boston Globe*, said: "You had men trolling, undergraduates ogling. You had small seedy men leaning on parking meters, eyeing and smoking, and people punching each other's lights out. It was a gamy playground for anyone interested in adventure of a certain kind. The Zone was nothing but sleaze." Teddy Venios, according to Howie Carr, better known by his underworld moniker 'Teddy Venus,' was the dominant figure in the Combat Zone from the 1960s until the early '80s. He paid off Mafia boss Gennaro Angiulo for protection and operated a string of 'clubs' with his brothers" Louie and Larry Venios. By 1974, in an attempt to contain the spread of these adult businesses, especially into Chinatown, the Boston Redevelopment Authority at the behest of Mayor Kevin H. White officially designated the Combat Zone as the city's adult entertainment district, and it was exempted from the usual ban on flashing neon signs, so the bright lights of the Combat Zone beckoned Bostonians nightly.

In this book, *The Other Red Line: Washington Street from Scollay Square to the Combat Zone*, I have tried to chronicle, in photographs, the evolution of Scollay Square in the early nineteenth century, and its evolution as an entertainment district in the mid-nineteenth century from the Howard Athenaeum, transformed from a temple of worship to a temple of burlesque that had vaudeville stars such as John Wilkes Booth, Charlotte Cushman, Lydia Thompson, Joseph Hart and John L. Sullivan, and later the Ladies of Scollay Square such as Sally Rand, Ann Corio, Gypsy Rose Lee, and a panoply of strippers, many of whom ironically adopted Boston Brahmin surnames and who entertained in the mid-twentieth-century Honey Alden, Belle Ayer, Faith Bacon, Candy Cotton, Betty Howard, Jenny Lee, Cookie Shaw, Honey Standish, and Barbara Curtis who was ironically billed as "The Proper Bostonian." As Scollay Square's allure waned in the late 1950s, that of the Combat Zone took on a new shine in the 1960s, albeit a tawdry and garish shine that tried to emulate the other but quickly devolved into a seedy, gritty place that offered vulgar and graphic entertainment.

This book on *The Other Red Line* was suggested by Bradley Jay, the popular host of *Jay Talking* on WBZ Radio/i Heart Media. I often appeared on his midnight talk show to discuss the many aspects of Boston history, not just from the early settlement in 1630 by Puritans seeking religious freedom, the Boston Tea Party, and the Great Molasses Flood, but also to discuss the shared memories of fellow Bostonians of now closed department stores, businesses, restaurants, and the once popular venues such as the Enchanted Village of Saint Nicholas at Jordan Marsh Department Store. On one of these shows, it was suggested by Bradley Jay that we do a segment on the Combat Zone, and from that suggestion evolved this book. History should always include the local likes, or dislikes, and the many shared memories of the city and hopefully this book will offer a glimpse into our memories of the entertainment districts of Boston that once not only attracted our attention, but that of our fathers, grandfathers, and even great grandfathers.

Oh! How I miss when I reminisce;
the friendly ways of those by-gone days.
Poor burlesque, how the populace frowned;
at women who danced and became ungowned.

Mike Gilmore

1

EARLY SCOLLAY SQUARE

Scollay Square, seen in in the early 1940s, looking west from the subway kiosk at Court Street, was a bustling area during the day and a destination at night. Alison Arnold of the *Boston Globe* said that "Early in the 20th century, Scollay Square began to deteriorate. Cheap restaurants, tattoo parlors, penny arcades, pawn shops and saloons gave it a raucous atmosphere." In essence, Scollay Square was long considered to be the "Times Square" of Boston and was a place that not only Bostonians frequented, but seemed to be the destination of every sailor docking in Boston. (*Author's collection*)

The Scollay Building was in the center of Scollay Square, which was named for William Scollay who directed the stagecoaches arriving and departing Boston from this building. The square had Court Street on the north and Treemont Row on the south with a large area between them. The Boston Athenaeum was located in this building from 1807 to 1809. In 1838, the area was officially named Scollay Square by the city and in 1856 horse-drawn streetcars replaced omnibuses. On the far right is the S.S. Pierce & Company store at Court and Tremont Streets, and on the right are two streetcars headed towards Chelsea. (*Courtesy of Joann Gricus*)

Looking north from Court Street, on the right, Scollay Square had numerous doctor and dental offices as well as sundry shops selling everything from dry goods, hats, musical instruments, and daguerreotype and ambrotype studios. The tall building in the center is the Sears Block, at the corner of Cornhill, which was built by David Sears in 1848 as a four-story commercial block. Restored by Don Stull Associates in 1969, it was added to the National Register of Historic Places in 1986 and is one of the few buildings to survive in Scollay Square.

The Howard Athenaeum opened in 1845 and on opening night, the *Boston Courier* said: "The Howard Athenaeum, a new candidate for patronage of the public, will be open tonight with a capital bill. The old tabernacle has been transformed into a very convenient and handsome theatre and it would sadly puzzle a Millerite to imagine himself at home in its now tasteful interior." The theater was designed by Isaiah Rogers in the Gothic Revival style and had 1,600 seats in orchestra, dress circle, gallery, and boxes. On opening night the play *School for Scandal*, a comedy of manners written by Richard Brinsley Sheridan in 1792, was performed, the same play as at the Boston Theatre in 1794, which broke the anti-theater law of theatrical performances in Boston.

As Rome points proudly to her Coliseum
So Boston treats her Howard Athenaeum

Reverend William Miller was a Baptist minister who is credited with beginning the mid-nineteenth-century religious movement, and he was the pastor of the Millerite Temple on Howard Street that later became the Howard Athenaeum. Miller had predicted the end of the world basing his calculations principally on Daniel 8:14: "Unto two thousand and three hundred days; then shall the sanctuary be cleansed" as the Earth's purification by fire at Christ's Second Coming. After the failure of Miller's expectations for October 22, 1844, the date became known as the Millerites' Great Disappointment.

A bronze statue of Governor John Winthrop, by Richard Greenough, was placed on a red granite pedestal in the center of Scollay Square in 1880 to commemorate the 250th anniversary of the settlement of Boston by the Puritans from England seeking religious freedom. On the right is Tremont Row, which extended along the east slope of Pemberton Hill facing Scollay Square as a row of commercial buildings with shops on the ground floor and small businesses above. On the left is Court Street leading to the Suffolk County Court House in Pemberton Square.

On the south side of Scollay Square, the junction of Court and Tremont Streets, was the Mercantile Building and the seven-story Hemenway Building, which was designed by the architectural firm of Bradlee, Winslow, and Wetherell and built for the Hemenway Trust in 1883. S.S. Pierce & Company was the first tenant of this building, having been at this corner since its founding in 1831, and they continued to occupy the ground floor until expanding to the Back Bay in 1887. On the far right is a corner of Tremont Row.

Looking north from the Governor Winthrop statue in 1890, the hubbub of Scollay Square was incredible with a parade of streetcars in a procession connecting one part of the city with others and horse-drawn delivery wagons supplying the numerous shops. In 1887, electric trolleys were introduced and would crisscross the city and connect the suburbs. On the far right is the Crawford House, "Where your Father and Grandfather enjoyed themselves for 50 Years," and the Oriental Tea Company with its famous "Steaming Tea Kettle."

Though the statue of Governor Winthrop commemorated the first governor of Massachusetts Bay Colony in the 1630s, it was placed in an awkward position as traffic concerns increased and it was moved first to Court Street facing the Old State House and then again in 1904 to the First Church, now First and Second Church, in the Back Bay to make room for the first head house of the underground subway. The streetcar on the right, which connected Boston with Central Square in Cambridge, was one of dozens of streetcars that connected the city to outlying neighborhoods and cities and towns.

The impressive Scollay Square Station kiosk replaced the Governor Winthrop statue when the underground subway was completed in 1898. The circular kiosk in the foreground is Court Street on the East Boston Tunnel connecting Maverick Square (present-day Blue Line), and the larger, more ornate one in the background is the Scollay Square Station on the Tremont Street Subway (today's Green Line.) The line was extended in 1916 to Bowdoin, and the Court Street Station was closed, and a new station was opened under the Scollay Square station and was called Scollay Under.

Cornhill, which was once the name of that part of Washington Street between School and Court Streets, was a curved Street that led from Scollay Square to Adams Square opposite Fanueil Hall. On the right is the Sears Crescent and on the left four-story commercial buildings, with the clock tower of the Leopold Morse Department Store projecting above the roof line.

With the Scollay Square Station kiosk on the right, this 1907 photograph of Scollay Square was a panoply of signs that advertised everything from watchmakers, dentists, hair salons, barber shops, photograph studios, cigar factories, and dozens of other small business concerns. The horse-drawn wagons are seen making deliveries. The Kingston Trio's song "MTA" has an appropriate line "Charlie's wife goes down to the Scollay Square Station, every day at quarter past two, and through the open window she hands Charlie a sandwich, as the train comes rumblin' through."

Looking south from Scollay Square in 1910, the Scollay Square Station kiosk is dwarfed by buildings on all three sides. In the center distance is the columned Boston City Hall Annex, the United States Trust Company, the Hemenway Building with S.S. Pierce & Company, and Tremont Row on the right with the Star Theatre and Scollay Square Olympia. (*Author's Collection*)

The Star Theatre opened in 1907 and was open from 9 a.m. to 11 p.m., and showed silent movies as short as twelve minutes as well as burlesque acts. The theater offered 10-cent admission with all seats being free, meaning no assigned seats. In the 1920s, it was renamed the Rialto Theatre, and in the 1930s, it earned its soubriquet "The Scratch House" as the theater was vermin infested from patrons who were not as fastidious in their hygiene as one might have hoped. The Rialto Theatre, which had been closed for repairs, reopened in 1951 as the only all-night movie house in Boston.

The Theatre Comique opened in 1906 as the first real motion picture theater in Boston. It offered on its marquee "For Man Woman and Child Continuous Performance New Features Weekly" from 1:30 p.m. to 10:30 p.m. and seats priced at a nickle for the balcony and 10 cents for orchestra. Its advertisement encouraged patrons to conveniently "Stay as Long as You Want." A typical program lasted a half hour, and consisted of a silent movie and several "illustrated songs," precursors to the "follow the bouncing ball" singalongs of later years performed by Mitch Miller.

The New Palace Theatre was
located on Court Street between
Hanover Street and Sudbury
Street and advertised as offering
the "Best Photo-Plays at All Times"
with Charlie Chaplin Comedies
weekly. However interesting the
entertainment, in a laboratory
in the dormered attic of this
building, Thomas Edison invented
his first patented invention, which
was the automatic vote counter,
and Alexander Graham Bell and
Thomas Watson first heard the
sound of a human voice over their
invention, the telephone.

The Scollay Square Olympia Theatre was in the center of what was left of Tremont Row and opened
in 1913 as a vaudeville theater. It was one of the places where Milton Berle, Fanny Brice, Fred Allen,
and many other vaudeville performers began their careers. Later, it switched to movies and is seen
advertising in 1947 *Blaze of Noon* with Anne Baxter and William Holden. Notice the Crescent Grill on
the right, which was famous for its barbecue chicken. (*Courtesy of John E. Lynes*)

The Scollay Square Olympia was a major theater in Boston and often hosted extravaganzas to accompany movie openings. Here, a horse-drawn stagecoach is drawn up in front of the theater as an advertisement for *Pioneer Trails*, a silent movie released in 1923 and featuring Cullin Landis, Alice Calhoun, and Bertram Grassby. The premise of the movie is "Jack is orphaned as a young child when his wagon train is ambushed by Indians. Twenty years later, he rescues Rose from a runaway stagecoach. The two fall in love, much to the displeasure of Blaney. To put him out of the way, Blaney kills Jack's adoptive mother and frames Jack for the crime."

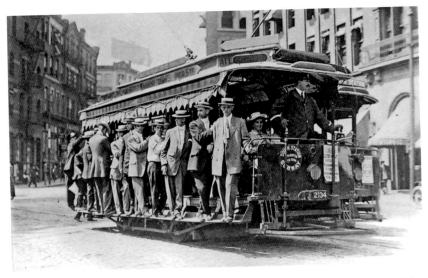

Scollay Square's accessibility from all parts of the city and suburbs as well as outlying cities and towns meant that a streetcar was bound to cross the square at one time or another. Streetcar 2134 is seen at Scollay Square connecting South Station and North Station with a full car and men standing on the running board.

2

EARLY VAUDEVILLE

Scollay Square, looking west, at the turn of the twentieth century was a bustling area of the city of Boston with Tremont Row on the left and Court Street on the right. Though really only a block in length, the square extended from Court Street, on the far right, to Cambridge Street in the distance. In the center, to the right of the policeman, is the Crawford House and to the right, the kiosk of the Sollay Square Station. On the left notice the "Opticians and Watchmakers" street clock. (*Courtesy of John E. Lynes*)

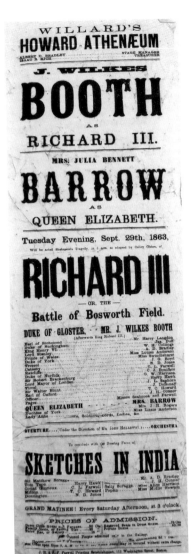

Above left: John Wilkes Booth was called "the handsomest man in America" and a "natural genius" and was noted for having an astonishing memory, which served him well in his stage career. The noted Civil War reporter George Townsend described him as a "muscular, perfect man" with "curling hair, like a Corinthian capital" and his stage performances were often characterized by his contemporaries as acrobatic and intensely physical, with him leaping upon the stage and gesturing with passion. Booth was billed as "The Pride of the American People, A Star of the First Magnitude," but his everlasting infamy was that he assassinated President Abraham Lincoln in 1865.

Above right: This 1863 broadside from the Howard Athenaeum featured John Wilkes Booth as Richard III, and Julia Bennett Barrow as Queen Elizabeth, in the Shakespearean tragedy *Richard II, or the Battle of Bosworth Field.* Booth was from a prominent theatrical family and his father Junius Brutus Booth and his brothers Junius Wilkes Booth and Edwin Booth, said to be the foremost Shakespearean tragedian actor of his day, were all prominent actors in the mid-nineteenth century.

Charlotte Saunders Cushman, on the left, and her sister Susan Webb Cushman performed at the Howard Athenaem in the Shakespearean play *Romeo and Juliet*. Cushman, with her distinctive voice noted for its full contralto register, was well-known for playing male characters, referred to as "breeches roles," such as Romeo, Hamlet, and Cardinal Wolsey and strong female characters like Lady Macbeth and Nancy Sykes in *Oliver Twist*. Tall, strikingly handsome, and highly charismatic, Cushman charmed theater patrons across two continents from the stage and her career lasted some four decades.

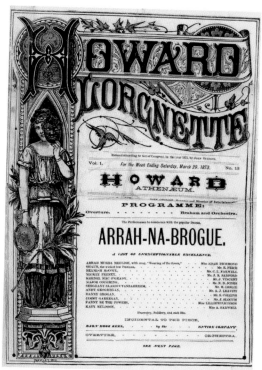

The Howard Lorgnette, Volume 1, No. 13, from 1873, advertised the drama *Arrah-Na-Brogue*, which is set during the Irish rebellion of 1798, and tells a story of love and loyalty under pressure and the action takes place over a forty-eight-hour period. Adah Richmond played Arrah Musha Mellish, who got her nickname "Arrah of the Kiss" when she helped Beamish McCoul escape from prison by concealing a message in her mouth and passing it to him in a kiss. The Irish nationalist play was by Dion Boucicault, the most successful playwright of the 1860s and was to become popular in theaters during the late nineteenth century.

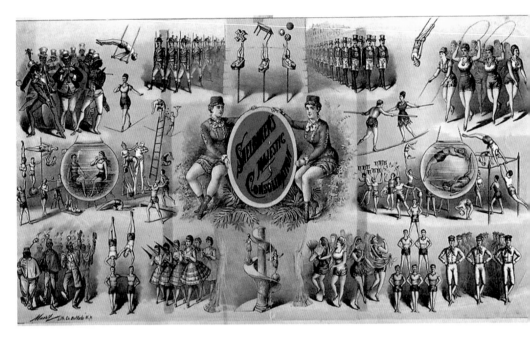

Above: Majestic Consolidation, produced by Snelbaker, was a popular production that had fifty performers of theater actors, acrobats, and comedians as a theatrical stage play with comedy vaudeville show. Among the performers were Ada Lynwood, Nellie Parker, Lillie Wood and Maggie Le Clair, Add Weaver, and Bob Allen. Since 1868, the Howard Athenaeum was "a variety-theatre, the leading and most successful house of its class." Often referred to as "the heart of American show business," vaudeville was to become one of the most popular types of entertainment in North America for several decades.

Left: The playbill for *Female 40 Thieves*, which was performed at the Howard Athenaeum, a "Novelty Theatre," in 1873 has on the cover two well-dressed women seated in their box with men standing behind them. In one corner, it has Hart and Stetson as proprietors and John Stetson as business manager of the theater. *Female 40 Thieves* was a pantomine with Adah Richmond playing Ganem and Lizzy Kelsey playing Hassarac, in an Ali Baba inspired all female cast, with a chorus of fifty voices. (*Author's collection*)

BRITISH BLONDE

BURLESQUE

TROUPE

Ledger Steam Job Print, Sixth and Chestnut Streets, Phila'd.

The British Blonde Burlesque Troupe was among the most popular entertainments during the 1860s and achieved great acclaim and notoriety. It was said that "The eccentricities of pantomime and burlesque, with their curious combination of comedy, parody, satire, improvisation, song and dance, variety acts, cross-dressing, extravagant stage effects, risqué jokes and saucy costumes, while familiar enough to British audiences, took the Howard Athenaeum audiences by storm. The British Blonde performers, rather than wearing layers of ruffles bared their stocking legs which was considered not just racy but risque. The sensation her burlesque troupe caused was unparalleled, a spectacle that inspired song and story."

Lydia Thompson, whose real name was Eliza Hodges Thompson, was considered the First Lady of Burlesque and was to introduce English burlesque to America where she was acclaimed for the dexterity of her dancing. Lydia Thompson is seen in the center holding a newspaper that might possibly hold a review of the burlesque act with the members of the British Blondes, who made no secret of their show's sex appeal. Newspaper ads never failed to mention the "Pretty Girls!" replete with capitalization and exclamation points, which was a boon for ticket sales.

An' way down front where the footlights glow
The bald headed men sat in the front row.
They had big glasses to see all the sights,
Including the blonds who dance in silk tights.

Above left: Adah Isaacs Menken, whose real name was Ada Berthe Theodore, was never considered a great actress but she had a flamboyance that did not go unnoticed. Said to be fearless, sensual, acrobatic, and gorgeous, all of which helped her land her big break, which was the lead in *Mazeppa*, a play based on a poem by Lord Byron about a seventeenth-century Cossack. "Although world-renowned because of her performance in *Mazeppa*, Menken's deepest desire was to be known as a serious poet," and would eventually publish a book of poetry in 1868, which she dedicated to the noted author Charles Dickens.

Above right: Haniola Kiralfy, seen bedecked with pearls and a feathered headdress, was a Hungarian who in the 1870s with her family would begin to produce grand spectacles that were performed not only at the Howard Athenaeum but in the major capitals of Europe; the stages were huge, the scenery unparalleled in scale, the special effects said to be eye watering. With her brothers Imre and Bolossy and her sisters Katie and Emily they were celebrated performers and the Kiralfy shows were live night after night and they were huge. One of their extravaganzas was *Around the World in Eighty Days*, by Jules Verne, that was a lavish stage set that propelled not just Haniola, but her family, to stardom.

Above left: Jennie Lee, whose real name was Emily Lee, was an English stage actress, singer, and dancer. Seen here dressed as Queen Naiad, in the fairy operetta by Emile Pacardo and Charles. F. Gordon, which she performed at the Boston Theatre where she also played Betsey Baker in a farce-comedy entitled, *The Wrong Man in the Right Place.* Burlesque performances rarely lasted more than an hour, which gave audiences just enough time to be enchanted by the extreme femininity of everything onstage, the dancing, the intriguing and evocative dialogue, minimal costuming, and loads of puns.

Above right: Pauline Markham, whose real name was Margaret Hale, was a noted dancer and contralto singer active on burlesque and vaudeville stages during the late nineteenth century. She was a member of the British Blondes, which had introduced Victorian burlesque to America, where for a few years she found phenomenal success. The critic Richard Grant White once described Markham's singing as "vocal velvet" and compared her arms to the lost arms of the Venus de Milo, which was incredible praise indeed. In *The Black Crook*, which featured Markham and other actresses attired in flesh-colored silk tights, she has been credited with starting "the great era of the leg show."

Above left: M. B. Leavitt's Gigantic Specialty Company brought Madame Eugenie Garretta, the "*Charmeuse de Pigeons*," for her first appearance in America to the Howard Athenaeum. Known as 'The European Sensation," Madame Garretta charmingly danced and performed with her well-trained pigeons, all the while dressed in a tight bustier corset, tights, and leather boots. To the dismay of late Victorian Bostonians, it was only for a one-week show but was advertised as "A Combination Without A Parallel!"

Above right: Sylvia Gray became known for her performances in burlesque shows such as *Monte Cristo Jr.* and *Little Jack Sheppard*, *Miss Esmeralda*, and *Ruy Blas and the Blase Roue*. In addition to appearing on stage, Gray also taught dance to actors and to wealthy clients, some of whom were drawn from the aristocracy, and among her many prominent students was Ellen Terry, who played every major Shakespearean role opposite the greatest British tragedians in England and in America.

Alma Stanley, whose real name was Lenore
Alma Stuart Stanley, had a career of more
than thirty years. She appeared in some sixty
plays and made two North American tours. In
1880, Stanley signed with M. B. Leavitt's Grand
English Operatic Burlesque Company and
performed in the United States as Pasquillo to
Selina Dolaro's Carmen in Frank W. Green's
Carmen or, Soldiers and Sevilleians.

Camille Andre was known as the Magic
Forest Queen and is seen with a bejeweled
kokoshnik tiara from which wired Shamrocks
radiate, and she holds a staff with a shamrock
finial and shamrocks wired along shaft.
A popular burlesque theater actress in the
early twentieth century, Andre's gown was
lavishly embroidered with shamrocks, which
by definition is a young sprig of clover, and she
performed a Celtic woodland dance.

Virginia Earle, whose surname was Earl, was a stage actress known for her work in light operas, Edwardian musical comedies and vaudeville over the decades surrounding the turn of the twentieth century. A review from 1900 described Earle as being without a rival "in the present stage of her artistic development" and her performance in a revival of *The Belle of New York* was said to be well received. In 1904, Earle performed at the Globe Theatre in *Sergeant Kitty*, a musical comedy where it was said she "has few equals as an arch and winsome singing soubrette." Among her best known performances was in the musicals *The Circus Girl* and *A Runaway Girl.*

Al Jolson, whose real name was Asa Yoelson, performed at the Old Howard in the early twentieth century, and was a popular singer whose performance of "Be My Baby Bumble Bee" launched him to success. By 1918, his career was ensured after he starred in the hit musical *Sinbad*, a "spectacular extravaganza in two acts and fourteen scenes" with music by Sigmund Romberg and Al Jolson, which became a hit Broadway musical. His famous song "Swanee" was added to the show and became composer George Gershwin's first hit recording. Jolson added "My Mammy," and by 1920, he had become the biggest star on Broadway. Three of Jolson's most popular songs were: "Toot, Toot, Tootsie," "California, Here I Come," and "April Showers." "My Buddy" was a popular song with music written by Walter Donaldson and lyrics by Gus Kahn, and in 1922 introduced by Al Jolson.

Joseph Hart, whose real name was Joseph Hart Boudrow, was the nephew of Josh Hart, who once managed Boston's Howard Athenaeum. Through his uncle, he played boy's parts in productions at the Old Howard, leading to a career in the professional theater. A popular vaudeville actor, one of the most notable of his revues would be the *Foxy Grandpa*, based on a popular comic strip created by Carl E. Schultze. He often played the rascally old gentlemen known as the "Foxy Grandpa," which was later to be reprised in two short films *The Boys Think They Have One on Foxy Grandpa* and *Foxy Grandpa and Polly in a Little Hilarity*.

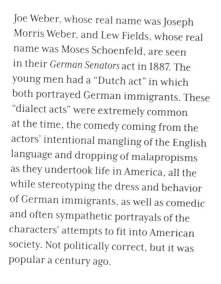

Joe Weber, whose real name was Joseph Morris Weber, and Lew Fields, whose real name was Moses Schoenfeld, are seen in their *German Senators* act in 1887. The young men had a "Dutch act" in which both portrayed German immigrants. These "dialect acts" were extremely common at the time, the comedy coming from the actors' intentional mangling of the English language and dropping of malapropisms as they undertook life in America, all the while stereotyping the dress and behavior of German immigrants, as well as comedic and often sympathetic portrayals of the characters' attempts to fit into American society. Not politically correct, but it was popular a century ago.

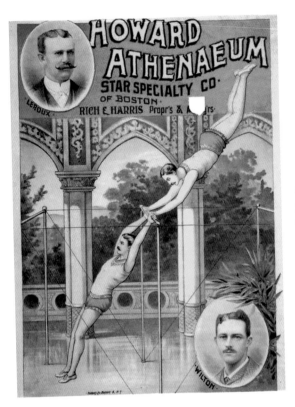

Charles Le Roux and George Wilton performed as gymnasts or trapeze artists swinging on bars as part of the Leroux and Wilton act at the Howard Athenaeum in 1887, sponsored by the Star Specialty Company. Joseph Johnson, whose stage name was Charles Le Roux, was never very well known, but his daring devilish sense of adventure eventually made him famous and inspired the sport of skydiving and as an inventor at heart who did much to improve his balloon and parachute. Unfortunately, he was killed in a parachuting accident in 1889 in Tallinn, Estonia.

JOHN L. SULLIVAN,
CHAMPION PUGILIST OF THE WORLD.
Born in Boston, October 15th 1858.

John L. Sullivan was known as the "Champion Pugilist of the World." Seen here in 1883, he was known as the "Boston Strong Boy" by the press and was an Irish-American boxer recognized as the first lineal heavyweight champion of gloved boxing, from 1882 to 1892. Sullivan often appeared in a skit at the Howard Athenaeum, and in boxing matches to the delight of the audience. Sullivan is considered the last bare-knuckle champion because no champion after him fought bare-knuckled and it was said "Do what we will with him, the man is a natural fighting animal."

3

DESTINATION SCOLLAY SQUARE

Scollay Square is just one short city block in a confluence of Boston streets. It is much more than just a geographical location or a row of buildings, it is a destination. Just ask any sailor whose ship has docked in Boston during World War II, the patrons of the clubs and bars, the bookies or the ladies of the evening where Scollay Square is and one might be surprised with the answer. Pearl Schiff said in her book *Scollay Square* that "Scollay Square is a mood, a rhythm ... that builds up to the grand finale at midnight when the doors open wide, spitting their customers into the street." (*Author's collection*)

Scollay Square was composed, according to Pearl Schiff, of "very few buildings which actually compromise the Square. A tavern, two movie houses, a sandwich bar a liquor store, a penny arcade, a cafeteria, a drugstore.... And across the street some more of the same, plus a few cafes where you can order a drink and see a floor show." With side streets such as Sudbury, Howard, Hanover, Brattle, Cornhill, and Court Streets acting as conduits to the nexus known as Scollay Square, there was a frenetic throb that drew its revelers nightly. On the left is D. W. Brennan Jewelry, Burke's Oldcourt Tavern, the Waldorf Cafeteria, and Sharaf's Restaurant. (*Courtesy of John E. Lynes*)

The Crawford House was opened in 1867 by Henry Goodwin and Henry Stumcke, and was operated on the European plan, where meals were not included and guests were welcome at its restaurant, bar, and theater. Relocating in 1874 to a new Gothic-inspired building designed by Joseph Richards in Scollay Square, the hotel had the Notch Dining Room, named for Crawford's Notch, which had a fine reputation. However, by the 1920s, it had in its Theatrical Bar numerous local dancers, musicians, and comedians and was to become well-known as the home of Sally Keith, a prominent burlesque performer in the city. On the left is the Oriental Tea Company with its famous steaming kettle as well as a tea-shaped sign board on the facade. The Crawford House was demolished in 1962 as part of the West End Urban Renewal.

The entrance to the Old Howard had three doorways with the polysemous saying above that clearly stated "Always Something Doing from 9:00 AM to 11:00 PM." The signboards of the Howard Athenaeum flank the entrances and advertise Diane Rowland, Tullah and Miy, and the Follies of the Day, which would be accompanied by Anthony DeSantis on the piano and in the evening orchestras. Orchestra and Dress Circle seats were 35 cents and balcony seats 25 cents. Notice the display case in the center with photographs of the Old Howard Queens of Burlesque.

The Howard Athenaeum, a veritable "Temple of Burlesque," was closed in 1953 when the Boston Vice squad made a film during one of their raids and captured the performance of "Irma the Body." This graphic film footage resulted in an indecency hearing, which eventually led to the closing of the Old Howard and because of the those charges, the city of Boston refused to renew the Old Howard's license after Judge Elijah Adlow ruled on them. The Old Howard was to remain closed for nearly a decade before being destroyed by fire in 1961. (*Courtesy of John E. Lynes*)

The Howard Athenaeum was designed by Isaiah Rogers and built in 1846 as a granite Gothic Revival theater, which offered a variety of theatricals, three penny operas, and vaudeville acts that were bawdy with burlesque. By 1893, it was presenting spectacles and dramas and would be renamed the Old Howard. During the Depression years, burlesque was the most popular form of entertainment offered across the country. Seen in a photograph from August 1953, Howard Street was thronged with men arriving for the performances of Carol Shannon, Betty Biddle, Toni Brennan, Mary Murray, and Dallas. (*Author's collection*)

> *Boston has two Athenaeums, both on Beacon Hill.*
> *One is for scholars with books by the score*
> *The other for lads who seek life in the roar.*
> *The Boston Athenaeum's lights are bright*
> *But the Howard Athenaeum's locked up tight*
> *Some Purist got himself a Jurist*
> *And slapped a padlock on the door*
> *Some Coward Closed the Old Howard.*

Frank W. Hatch

Joe and Nemo was established in 1909 and known from coast to coast as the "Dog Kings." The restaurant was on Howard Street and was named for Joe Merlino and Anthony "Nemo" Caloggerom and their restaurant served a variety of foods, but they became renowned for their hot dogs, which were made from a special formula by the New England Provision Company. The hot dogs were cooked in water and the buns steamed and were often served "all around," meaning that it was served with mustard, relish, onions, and horseradish. By the 1960s, there were over two dozen Joe and Nemo restaurants, serving a million hot dogs annually. (*Courtesy MIT Libraries*)

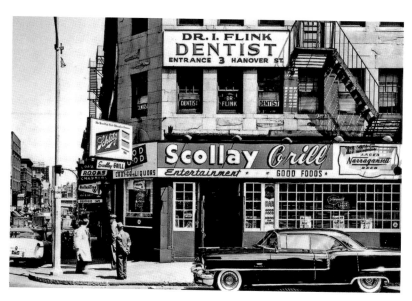

The Scollay Grill was at the corner of Court and Hanover Streets. Offering not just good food but entertainment, with "booths for ladies," its strategic location in Scollay Square made it a destination before and after the bars. Above was the dental office of Dr. Isadore Flink. Scollay Square was one of the few neighborhoods on Boston where one could get a drink, a tattoo, and dental work all done on the same block. (*Courtesy MIT Libraries*)

The Red Hat is on Bowdoin Street, just west of Scollay Square and is the last of the many bars that once offered libations in and around Scollay Square. Opened in 1907 the Red Hat catered to sailors on leave, dockworkers and shipbuilders looking for an inexpensive place to eat, but soon became a local favorite to businessmen on their lunch hour. Today, the "Red Hat is a rare reminder of Boston's yesteryear, bringing an earthy spice to the more refined palate of Beacon Hill—an unpretentious watering hole to gain some courage for the climb."

The Tasty was at the corner of Court and Hanover Streets and advertised "For good Hot Dogs and Hamburgers visit the Tasty Lunch." The Tasty was owned and operated by Cleanthe Valacellis who was an immigrant in 1910 from Lesbos. The Tasty in Scollay Square was the first of eventually four restaurants that he opened around Boston. On the second floor was the Scollay Tattoo Shop, opened in 1909 by Ed "Dad" Liberty and continued by his son Harold "Lefty" Liberty, which was the last tattoo parlor in Scollay Square. (*Author's collection*)

Looking west on Scollay Square in 1950, the marquees of the Rialto Theatre and the Olympian Scollay Square Theatre, with a huge clock surmounted billboard above the Scollay Square Half Dollar Saloon, which happened to be blank that day. On the right is the Crawford Bar and Grill and to its left the Theatrical Bar featuring Ann Castle and Dancing Beauties. David Kruh said in his book *Always Something Doing* that Scollay Square "was a place geared almost solely for amusement." There were many of sailors from around the world who once thought of liberty in Boston as only to be celebrated in Scollay Square. (*Courtesy MIT Libraries*)

The neon sign of the Amusement Centre in Scollay Square not only offered photomatic pictures and a shooting gallery, but ladies were invited and admission was free. This was a place that had coin-operated machines, pinball machines, slots, gumball machines, and among the popular games were Baffle Ball and Flipper Bumpers. Opened in 1942 as a penny arcade, and with not only coin-operated machines, a shooting gallery, a variety of entertainment, and a photo booth, it was also more than just entertainment, but a warm place on a cold evening. (*Courtesy MIT Libraries*)

Looking towards Scollay Square along Hanover Street, the Rialto Theatre and the Scollay Square Olympian Theatre are seen in the distance. On the right can be seen the Pisa Italian Home Kitchen Restaurant and the Stage Door Cafe. The Carnival Cafe at Cornhill was a popular bar with shows every evening. (*Courtesy MIT Libraries*)

Cornhill, on the left, was a gently curved street that led from Scollay Square to the front of Fanueil Hall. The Sears Block was at the corner with the Court Street Tavern on the ground floor and Salvy's Barber Shop above. The Sears Block was built in 1848 by David Sears, a leading mid-nineteenth-century developer who also built the Sears Crescent adjacent to it. The Sears Block is now the location of the "Steaming Tea Kettle", an 1873 trade sign of the Oriental Tea Company that was located on their building on Scollay Square demolished in 1967 during the construction of Government Center.

An enormous billboard advertising Narraganset Lager Beer rises above the Fitz Inn Auto Park, with Jack's Lighthouse Bar and its prominent three-dimensional Narraganset beer lighthouse on the facade, with its famous Bar-B-Q Chicken advertised, and the Tasty on the right. Notice the "Old Stag" beer delivery truck in front, which had been brewed in Illinois since 1851. (*Courtesy MIT Libraries*)

Seen in the late 1950s, Tremont Street looking towards Scollay Square had on the left the Odessa Restaurant, Waggy's Delicatessen and the Storyland Bar. On the corner is the Suffolk Savings Bank with its monumental granite columns is facing Simpson's Loan Company in the distance. On the right is Cobb's Restaurant which had been founded in 1860 and famous for seafood, sirloin steak, and filet mignon. (*Courtesy MIT Libraries*)

The Salvation Army anchored this corner of Scollay Square between Sudbury and Hanover Streets and in the distance can be seen the two-story lighthouse of Jack's Lighthouse Bar. On the left are Ferrara's Grille, Bill's Bar-B-Q, Dixie's Bar, and the Belmont House that offered rooms by the day or week. (*Courtesy MIT Libraries*)

The Howard Casino Theatre was on Hanover Street close to Scollay Square and featured the Follies. Opened in 1910, with a 1,300-seat capacity, it offered a new show every Monday by the early 1960s, and advertised as "Boston's only girly show." In 1962, the Howard Casino was packed for the last show. Box seats which usually went unsold were filled early, and when the first attractions scampered into the spotlight there was standing room only. Choruses of "Pop Goes the Weasel," "Coming Through the Rye," "Smoke Gets in Your Eyes," and several varieties of the "Twist" were performed, which received shouts of "Take it off" before the place was closed. On the left is Johnny Martin's Burley Lounge. (*Author's collection*)

Looking south from Howard Street, Scollay Square's signage made it one of the more frenetic business areas of the city of Boston. Shops include Paul's Barber Shop, Goldman's Clothes for Men, the Belmont House, the Royal Café, and Dixie's Bar. Notice the tower of the New England Telephone Company rising above the buildings, and to the left of the Pepsi Cola truck can be seen the cupola of the Old West Church. (*Courtesy MIT Libraries*)

The east side of Scollay Sqare had the Crawford House with its marquee above advertising a performance by Ann Castle and the Dancing Beauties. The huge clock surmounted billboard is advertising the popular soft drink company Cott, "It's Cott to be good!" Cott Beverage Corporation was founded in 1923 by Solomon Cott and distributed seventeen flavors of tonic. In the distance can be seen the Art Deco New England Telephone Building at Bowdoin Square. (*Courtesy MIT Libraries*)

The Hotel Imperial Grill was on Cambridge Street between Scollay and Bowdoin Squares and was advertised as "Where old Friends meet," such as the Marine and Sailor who greet one another by shaking hands. It was said that "From Zanzibar to Calcutta From Liverpool to the Arctic Circle ... wherever servicemen gather... you'll find the men we've entertained in Boston!" and with four bars, seating for 700, dancing, good food, and snappy entertainment, it was immensely popular. (*Author's collection*)

The Half Dollar Bar, which claimed to be "Known From Coast to Coast," was at the corner of Cambridge and Sudbury Streets facing Scollay Square, offering Pickwick Ale on its sign. A cachet the bar was that actual half dollar coins were embedded in the wood of the bar top, and one can only imagine the consternation of the inebriated patron trying to pay his tab with one. On the left is Goldman's Clothes for Man "On the Square." (*Author's collection*)

The Tasty and the Scollay Bar and Grill flank Hanover Street that once extended from Scollay Square to Commercial Street on the waterfront and is one of the oldest streets in Boston. On the left of Hanover Street is the Casino Theatre and on the right the Crawford Chambers. The Casino Theatre was a burlesque house featuring burlesque dancers and between acts feature films were shown, probably to allow the audience to cool down. (*Courtesy MIT Libraries*)

In the early 1950s, the Rialto Theatre advertised as "Boston's All-Nite Theatre," seen on the right, was flanked by M. Leventhal Jeweler and the Tattoo Studio of Professor Oscar Bouchard, a man who was said to be inked from head to toe, and was a master at electric tattooing until 1962, when Massachusetts banned the trade; notice the sign for the bowling alley in the basement.

By the late 1950s, Scollay Square had become a seedy, run down neighborhood. On the left is the closed Eastern Labor Agency, the Hub Bar-B-Q, a Surplus Warehouse, Leventhal's Jeweler, the Rialto Theatre, and the Scollay Square Olympia. By the early 1960s, Scollay Square faded and accrording to Robert Taylor "its death knell did not find us throbbing with nostalgia." (*Courtesy MIT Libraries*)

On the left is the Suffolk Savings Bank on the opposite corner Epstein's Drug Store with an enormous billboard advertising the new headquarters of the Merchants Co-Operative Bank. Court Street led to Pemberton Square with the Suffolk County Courthouse (now called John Adams Courthouse), designed by George Clough and built in 1885. By 1895, a few of the elegant swell bay facade red brick row houses remained on Pemberton Square but were used as public and law offices, and it was also the site of the Boston Police Headquarters, the Boston Conservatory of Elocution, Oratory, Dramatic Art (later Emerson College), and the Horace Mann School for the Deaf. (*Courtesy MIT Libraries*)

Looking towards Pemberton Square from Scollay Square, the impressive Suffolk County Courthouse commands the view. Built in 1893, the courthouse was designed by George A. Clough, the first city architect of the city of Boston, as a monumental Second Empire design, which was his largest and most elaborate design. In 1909, Clough enlarged the building with a French Chateau-style roof, which added two stories. On the right is Epstein's Drug Store and the Pemberton Shoe Repair and Shine Shop and on the left the Suffolk Savings Bank. (*Courtesy of John E. Lynes*)

Looking east from Scollay Square, Court Street leads towards the Old State House. On the left is Patten's Restaurant which was famous for native New England dishes and fresh seafood that were served in the Grill Room and Georgian Room on the ground floor, and the Early American Room upstairs. Some of the foods were uniquely Boston such as the sliced egg, tomato and potato chip salad, and for dessert squash pie and coffee jello. On the left the United States Trust Company and the new locatioon of Epstein Drug Store on the ground floor of the Hemenway Building. (*Author's collection*)

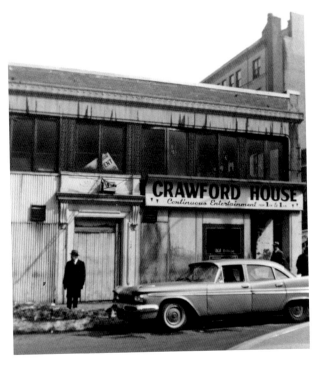

The Crawford House had by 1962 become a shell of its once impressive facade. In 1926, the portion of the Crawford House facing Court Street was taken by eminent domain by the city of Boston to widen Cambridge and Court Streets, and the facade was demolished. After a fire in 1948, the third through sixth floors of the hotel were demolished, but the first and second floors were retained and the Theatrical Bar was kept open. It offered continuous entertainment from 1 p.m. to 1 a.m., but it never was as popular when Sally Rand twirled her tassels in the Crawford House's Theatrical Bar. (*Author's collection*)

The Government Center Station replaced the Scollay Square Station and its kiosks, being located on the site of Cornhill on Boston City Hall Plaza. These three people probably saw the changes that had taken place in Scollay Square in the twentieth century and point out once-famous locations. The red brick building in the distance is the Sears Crescent built in 1816 as commercial buildings, which in 1862 had the facades unified with Italianate detailing and lintels. (*Courtesy of Frank Cheney*)

4

SCOLLAY SQUARE RIALTO

The ethereal Sally Rand was a well-known performer who began her career as an acrobatic dancer at carnivals in the Ringling Brothers and Barnum and Bailey Circus. Rand was a graceful and refined burlesque dancer and would play peek-a-boo with her body by manipulating huge ostrich fans both in front and behind her, and like a winged bird she would swoop and twirl on the stage as "a guard to keep too much of mother nature from showing." She often performed to the delight of her audience to the classic tune by Claude Debussy "Au Clair de la Lune."

Though this is not quite the Vincent Club Drill, the Howardettes of the Old Howard seem to have it down pat! The Howardettes were a group of chorus dancers, seen here in sweet but sexy Little Bo Peep costumes with a ruffled collar and an ostrich feathered hat, and they would perform a line dance with a high kick to the delight of the audience. The choreography of the Howardettes, which was considered the infinity of expression, was staged by Madeline Mixon and the fetching costumes were by Eva Collins.

Sophie Tucker, whose real name was Sofya Kalish, was well known for her powerful delivery of comical and risqué songs and was one of the more popular entertainers in America during the first half of the twentieth century. She was widely known by the monikor "The Last of the Red Hot Mamas," as her hearty sexual appetite was a frequent subject of her songs. Tucker began integrating "fat girl" humor, which became a common thread in her acts and her popular songs included "I Don't Want to Get Thin" and "Nobody Loves a Fat Girl, But Oh How a Fat Girl Can Love." Jack Yellen wrote one of her most famous songs, "My Yiddishe Momme." The song was often performed in large American cities where there were sizable Jewish audiences.

Fred Allen, whose real name was John Florence Sullivan, became a regular on the burlesque circuit and used a variety of gimmicks in his changing act, from a ventriloquist dummy to juggling and singing, but the focus was always on his comedy, which was heavy on wordplay. He adopted his stage name, Fred Allen, to honor the Revolutionary War hero Ethan Allen who, he wittily noted, was no longer using the name. Allen's wit was at times not intended for the vaudeville audience but rather for other professionals in show business. After one of his performances fell flat one day, Allen made the best of it by circulating an obituary of his act on black-bordered mourning stationery. He later hosted *The Fred Allen Show*, which made him one of the most popular and forward-looking humorists in the Golden Age of American radio.

In between skits at the Old Howard, a few of the Howardettes in their costumes would often knit to while away the time between their three performances daily as they sit on an unused piano. These performances included not just practice time and learning new routines, but were rigorous stage acts with dance and often singing. What better way to spend one's free time by mending costumes, sewing new ones, or to relax by knitting a scarf or hat and chatting?

Phil Silvers was a popular vaudeville actor and was an entertainer and comedic actor known as "The King of Chutzpah." Seen here he is backstage at the Old Howard chatting with Tempest Storm between acts. As a teenager, he was working as a singer in the Gus Edwards Revue, and then worked in vaudeville and as a burlesque comic. Silvers scored a major triumph in *Top Banana*, a Broadway show of 1952 in which he played Jerry Biffle, the egocentric, always-busy star of a major television show and won a Tony Award for his performance.

Ray Bolger, whose real name was Raymond Wallace Bolger, was a vaudevillian, singer, tap dancer, and stage performer who began his career in a vaudeville tap show, creating the act "Sanford & Bolger a Pair of Nifties" with his dance partner Ralph Sanford. He eventually went into theater and movies and is immortalized as the Scarecrow in the movie the *Wizard of Oz*. In fact, Bolger's Scarecrow is ranked among the "most beloved movie characters of all time" by AMC and the American Film Institute.

Jimmy Durante, whose real name was James Francis Durante, was a popular vaudeville performer whose clipped gravelly speech, Lower East Side New York accent, comic language-butchery, jazz-influenced songs, and prominent nose helped make him one of America's most familiar and popular personalities from the 1920s through the 1970s. He often referred to his nose as the *schnozzola*, an Italianization of the American Yiddish slang word *schnoz*, meaning big nose. Durante would team with Garry Moore for *The Durante-Moore Show* and Durante's comic chemistry with the young, brush cut Moore brought Durante an even larger audience. "Dat's my boy dat said dat!" became Durante's catchphrase.

Faith Bacon, whose real name was Frances Yvonne Bacon, was a popular burlesque dancer who was billed as "America's Most Beautiful Dancer" and during her career she used bubbles, flowers, fake swans, and ostrich feather fans in her almost-nude dance routines. Performing her erotic fan dance, which she claimed to have originated and which was as elegant as her dance was artistic, across America, she caused a literal sensation both among the public and the police. The fan dance took off, and in 1933, she would create a sensation with her "Dance of Shame," in the process of competing with the better-known Sally Rand who is reputed to have plagiarized a portion of Bacon's routines. Faith Bacon, in regards to her immense popularity, said "Try to get yourself arrested as much as possible."

Above left: Sherry Britton, whose real name was Edith Zack, was 5 feet 3 inches tall and had an 18-inch waist, and was once said to have a "figure to die for." She got her stage name from a bottle of Harvey's Bristol Cream Sherry, though it is not recorded whether it was sweet or dry sherry, let alone Amontillado. During World War II, she toured hospitals and entertained wounded soldiers and Franklin Delano Roosevelt bestowed upon her the rank of honorary brigadier general for her volunteer work. Britton was said to be innately classy and stripped to classical music, wearing lovely long gowns often with glittering tiaras.

Above right: Ann Corio, whose surname was originally Coiro and was changed because her family disapproved of her chosen profession, was a popular burlesque stripper and actress. Corio's good looks and shapely figure landed her showgirl roles that led to her becoming a well-known striptease artist. Her popularity as a featured performer on the burlesque circuit began at The Old Howard where she became "Harvard's Baby," beloved by Harvard students and the Harvard class of 1937 even made her an honorary member. In 1962, she created an off-Broadway show, *This Was Burlesque,* which she directed and in which also performed and later wrote a book with the same title on her life as a burlesque icon.

A woman's greatest asset is a man's imagination.

Ann Curio

Sally Rand, whose real name was Helen Gould Beck, was an American burlesque dancer, vedette, and actress, most noted for her ostrich feather fan dance and balloon bubble dance. It was said that Cecil B. DeMille gave her the name Sally Rand, inspired by a Rand McNally atlas. She was noted for her fan dance that she would perform to such music as Claude Debussy's "Clair de Lune" and Frédéric Chopin's "Waltz in C Sharp Minor," which never ceased to create a sensation and which sustained her career that would last for more than three decades.

I confess that I am a brazen hussy, if out-of-shape women want to call me that.

Sally Rand

Sally Keith, whose real name was Stella Katz, was a well-known performer at The Crawford House where she was popularly known as "The Queen of the Tassel Tossers" and where she had a drink named after her—the Tassel Tosser, a combination of brandy, anisette and triple sec, hopefully served over ice. Sally Keith performed at The Crawford House's Theatrical Bar in Boston's Scollay Square for two decades. Her renowned specialty was to twirl two tassels on her breasts and two on her buttocks, and she was highly skilled at being able to twirl them in every direction, especially opposite. Keith was celebrated as making those tassels spin with a fury, to the delight of her audience. Keith also composed a song "Belittling Me," which was published as sheet music.

Gypsy Rose Lee, whose real name was Rose Louise Hovick, was a famous vedette and burlesque stripper. Her innovations were an almost casual stripping style compared to the herky-jerky styles of most burlesque strippers, and she emphasized the "tease" in "striptease," and brought a sharp sense of humor into her act as well. She became as famous for her onstage wit as for her stripping style, and changed her stage name to Gypsy Rose Lee. Lee viewed herself as a "high-class" stripper and dressed in elegant but risqué outfits and her style of intellectual recitation while stripping was to be spoofed in the number "Zip!" in Rodgers and Hart's *Pal Joey*. She later penned a novel, *The G-String Murders*, published by Simon & Schuster in 1941.

Joan Shawlee, also known as Joan Fulton, was a popular performer and billed as Joyce Ring, she performed in the Broadway productions *By Jupiter* (1942) and *A Connecticut Yankee* (1943.) The adjective "statuesque" is often applied to Shawlee. In the early 1960s, Shawlee and actress Mitzi McCall formed a team to perform as a night club act. In January 1961, syndicated newspaper columnist Dorothy Kilgallen reported that the duo was "causing quite a stir," and she cited the partners' discrepancy in height with "Joan being six feet, three inches tall and Mitzi four feet, ten inches short."

Rosita Royce, whose real name was Marjorie Rose Corrington, was known for her famous "Doves of Peace Dance." It was said of her stage act that Rosita entered fully clothed, wearing long velvet gloves. Within minutes, her father released seven doves who landed on Rosita's gloved arms, shoulders, and head. Each bird weighed 14 pounds, which was nearly three times the size of ordinary pigeons. As the music played, Miss Royce called each bird by their name (whose names have not been recorded) who then carefully and adroitly removed a piece of her costume. She later became an actress and starred in *Sunset Strip* and, somewhat ironically, in the movie *Striporama*.

Zorita the Snake Dancer, whose real name was Kathryn Boyd, was a burlesque dancer who was best known for a dance in which she performed with two slithering boa constrictors that she named "Elmer and Oscar" and which was considered to be the biggest draw the Old Howard ever had. These snakes were a gift to her from a snake charmer friend, and she included them as part of her unique act until she was arrested by the American Society for the Prevention of Cruelty to Animals for the use of the snakes in her act. Zorita became well-known for her unique and controversial performances such as the "Half and Half," in which she dressed one half of her body as a groom and the other as a bride, and, keeping one side to the audience, began to undress each other, leading to the inevitable "wedding night romp."

Georgia Sothern, whose real name was Hazel Anderson, was a burlesque dancer and vaudeville performer who might have been one of the most statuesque strippers at the Old Howard. Southern was quite a stripper and "As the orchestra blasted, she tossed her body, flipping it forward and back, cranking her neck high and low." She was known for her striptease performances often opening her act with the song "Georgia On My Mind," and became so popular that during a performance in 1939 at the Old Howard in Boston, she gave an interview to the *Harvard Crimson*, to the delight of her many Harvard undergraduate admirers; *The New York Times* called her "unpretentiously hot stuff."

Yvonne De Carlo, whose real name was Margaret Yvonne Middleton, was often a contestant in beauty contests and later worked as a dancer in nightclubs where she had a popular "King Kong" number (seen here with Emil Van Horn) in which she danced and cast off several chiffon veils before being carried away by the gorilla, who awaited his cue while standing in the wings. With numerous stage and screen credits, it was in 1956 that Cecil B. DeMille cast her as Zipporah, the wife of Moses, played by Charlton Heston, in his biblical epic *The Ten Commandments*, a Paramount Pictures production. However, many people will also fondly remember her as Lily Munster in the popular 1960s television show *The Munsters*.

Trudine, whose real name was Ruth Tropea, was the acknowledged "mistress of the striptease" and was popularly referred to as a "Danseuse Exotique." She got her nickname the "Queen of Quiver" because she could "stand in one spot on the stage of the Old Howard and without moving back and forth, get her whole body to quiver," to the absolute delight of the audience. Her scant working attire, in addition to a black G-string, included a net bra and sandals but she also performed with masses of feather fans to the delight of the audience.

Lois De Fee was called the Queen of the Amazons, where with her great 6 feet 4 inches of height (6 feet 8 inches in high heels) she performed at the New York World's Fair in 1939. She began a career in burlesque and it was Sherry Britton who taught her the subtle art of stripteasing, and was obviously an exemplary student as she later went on to be a top-grossing headliner throughout the 1940s and into the 1950s. Walter Winchell called De Fee, with her great height, the "Eiffel Eyeful."

Princess Lohoma, whose real name was Lahoma Willingham, was part Chickasaw Indian and born into a family that was very active in the affairs of the tribe. Lahoma's cousin, Floyd May Tubby was governor of the Chickasaw Nation, and in 1943, he appointed Lahoma as the "Chickasaw Princess" at the 1943 American Indian Exposition. In that capacity, she frequently represented the Chickasaw Nation in parades and at official gatherings. Princess Lahoma became one of the most popular feature burlesque dancers of the 1950s, often billed as "an exotic Indian dancer with a white teepee," and was among the highest paid burlesque dancers of her era.

Rose La Rose, whose real name was Rosina DePella, was a popular burlesque dancer called the "Most Spectacular Strip Teaser of them all," whose trademark was coming onto the stage elegantly dressed and singing the song to the audience "Who will kiss my Oo La La!" after which she would slap her "Oo La La fanny." La Rose, the "Dark Eyed Ball of Fire," was very popular and she would register two of her burlesque performances in 1950 with the Billboard Protection Bureau entitled *Boudoir Sensation* and *Park Beach Fantasy*. She later would produce a two-hour cabaret show called *Rose La Rose and her Sophisticated Rose Buds* in 1955. Among her movie credits were the *Queen of Burlesque*, *The Wages of Sin*, and *Sunset Strip*.

Betty Howard, whose real name was Betty Jean Howard, often referred to herself as the "Girl who has Everything" and the public adoringly called her "Betty Blue Eyes Howard." By saying she had "everything," Howard was referring to her breasts, all 40 inches worth. Bette Howard often appeared at the Old Howard, sharing the stage with Rose La Rose and Nona Carver. She was a star by the 1940s and would hit her stride in the 1950s, but not before she had a wide following of admirers.

Winnie Garrett was known as "The Raven Haired Beauty of Burlesque," as well as "The Flaming Redhead." She was famous for being a fast-stepping striptease dancer with her dance group the "Bomb-A-Dears" and would often appear in a $1,000 rhinestone sewn gown. Winnie was also referred to as the "Queen of the Peelers" and would dance to mostly up-tempo music. However, she had business acumen and she was the owner and song writer of two businesses, the Winnie Garret Recording Company "Famous Records" 1947 and Winnie Garret Music Publishing, and as a successful songwriter she wrote the hit tune "All Dressed Up and No Place to Go."

Tempest Storm, whose real name was Annie Blanche Banks, was a bombshell known for her fiery locks, her grinding hips, and her 44DD bust and is one of the most well-known and best-loved burlesque legends. One newspaper said that Tempest was a "Tempest in a D cup," and it was said that when she started in burlesque "The instant the spotlight hit, my gown fell off. I was still wondering whether I had the nerve take it off, and it fell off. So that was when I learned the basic rule in this business: No matter what happens, keep moving." Storm worked hard to attain her sensational physique; in the 1950s, she applied to Lloyd's of London to insure her "moneymakers," her ample breasts, for $1 million. She later appeared in two films, *Teaserama* and *Buxom Beautease*.

Carmella, whose real name was Carmella Torregrossa, was referred to as the "Sophia Loren of Burlesk" and noted for her dark Italian looks. Starting out in vaudeville theaters in the 1940s, by 1950, she had migrated to burlesque dance, originally dancing under the stage name "The Torrid Twister." Because of her remarkable resemblance to the sultry looks of Sophia Loren, she was nicknamed in her honor. Carmela was known for her muscle control and acrobatic style. She was also a talented seamstress and made all her own costumes, including the hand beading that embellished her gowns.

Kay Randall, seen here in just a mink stole and high heels, was referred to as the "O.K. Girl" when she danced at the Old Howard in the late 1950s and into the early 1960s. One assumes that "the O.K. Girl" is a play on her first name, or maybe it is just because she was originally from Oklahoma. Often, the Old Howard had the Torrid-Teaser Burlesquers as a prelude to the strip tease act.

Sally Lane was referred to as "Sally the Majestic." She would often be accompanied in her act by her little sidekick Fifi the Monkey in her act "Monkey Business." Fifi was was dressed in a leopard skin cape and leopard fez and was an integral part of her striptease act; Sally also performed with an Angora cat, but unfortunately her name has not been recorded. As was common place for Burlesque dancers she too was arrested for performing an "immoral dance" but Fifi might have slipped the charge because he was still wearing his fez.

Jenny Lee, whose real name was Virginia Lee Hicks, was a stripper, burlesque entertainer, and pin-up model who performed several striptease acts in nightclubs during the 1950s and 1960s. She was also known as "the Bazoom Girl" as her act centered on how fast she could get her pastie propellers to spin every which way and how dizzy she could make the audience who were watching her so intently. Lee was also known as "the Burlesque Version of Jayne Mansfield." Lee was a noted pin-up girl throughout her career, but like many of her contemporaries, she never posed nude. She established the Exotic World Museum, now known as the Burlesque Hall of Fame, that preserves the legacy of burlesque and its performers.

Blaze Starr, whose real name was Fannie Belle Fleming, was an American stripper and burlesque star and referred to as "Miss Spontaneous Combustion!" Her vivacious presence and inventive use of stage props earned her the nickname "The Hottest Blaze in Burlesque." She once acquired a baby Samoa leopard with the hope of working him into a stage act. Hiding small pieces of meat in her costume to train the leopard to paw at, and hence remove, from her costume. Unfortunately, the leopard proved a tad more hungry that evening and clawed at Blaze rather than as rehersed, which led to his swift retirement from the shortest animal career in showbiz. Blaze would be immortalized in the film *Blaze* starring Paul Newman, which was based on the 1974 memoir *Blaze Starr: My Life*.

Dixie Evans, whose real name was Mary Lee Evans, was a burlesque stripper who is best known for a burlesque parody in which she performed as Marilyn Monroe. Evans' "Marilyn Monroe" act was to become the dancer's trademark and it certainly went over big with audiences. One wonders if Dixie ever sang the famous song "Happy Birthday Mr. President" that the sultry and sexy Monroe, in a skin tight Jean Louis designed bejeweled gown, sang to John Fitzgerald Kennedy in 1962 on his forty-fifth birthday at Madison Square Garden. Kennedy said after the song "I can now retire from politics after having had Happy Birthday sung to me in such a sweet, wholesome way."

Rita Gomez was an exotic dancer in the late 1950s. She had the sultry and brooding look of her Latin blood and showed off her body in a bikini that had the top cut so low that her bejeweled pasties were evident. Seen here in a feathered cape, she danced and stripped as each rhinestone on her scanty outfit glittered in the stage lights.

Irma the Body, whose real name was Mary Elizabeth Goodneighbor, started her burlesque striptease career as a chorus dancer; when another stripper was on stage, the audience would boo that stripper and cheer for Irma who was dancing in the background. Irma became known as "Sophisticated Dynamite" and was considered both sultry and sexy to the extreme and in 1953 during one of her performances at the Old Howard in Boston she was charged with open and gross lewdness and taking part in an immoral show. Irma was arrested along with Rose La Rose and Marion Russell on indecency charges and all three ladies were each charged a $200 fine. Due to the indecency charges, the city of Boston refused to renew the Old Howard's license and the theater would remain empty for almost a decade.

Lily Ann Rose, whose real name was Lillian Kiernan, grew up in a vaudeville family known as the Patent Leather Girls, which was composed of her mother Margie and aunt Lillian. Lily Ann started in the chorus line of a risque burlesque show at the Casino Theater, and would become a protege of well-known dancer Sally Keith and performed a shadow act dacing with Sally in "Me and My Shadow." One of her acts was the "Girl in Gold," with her barely covered body covered in gold paint and she stood as still as a statue. Lily Ann was banned in Boston following an incident in which she almost "accidentally" bared her breasts while performing her opening night act on stage at the Old Howard.

5

WASHINGTON STREET STORES

Looking along Washington Street from West Street there were low-rise buildings that on the ground floor had numerous specialty shops and stores including Grayson's, the Holly Shop, Fanny Farmer Candies, Carlyle's, Richard's, S.S. Kresge's, Hudson's, Gilchrist Department Store, E. B. Horne Jewelers, I. J. Fox Furriers, Loew's Theatre, and W. T. Grant. Washington Street in the years before the advent of suburban shopping malls offered everything under the sun for shoppers, and then some. (*Author's collection*)

Left: Washington Street, between School and Court Street, was often referred to as Publisher's Row as there were numerous local newspapers located along the street among them the *Herald Traveler* on the left, the *Boston Globe* on the right, and the *Boston Post* on the right out of site. Notice the streetcars and horse-drawn delivery wagons, which with pedestrians often made the streets impassable.

Below: The Dr. Thomas Crease House and apothecary shop was at the corner of Washington and School Streets and was built in 1718; it is the oldest brick building in Boston. It was later the shop of Ticknor and Fields, a publisher of nineteenth-century American writers including Emerson, Nathaniel Hawthorne, Oliver Wendell Holmes, Henry Wadsworth Longfellow, Harriet Beecher Stowe, and Henry Thoreau. By the late 1950s, it had become the King of Pizza Shop, at 15 cents a slice, with its facade masked by signs and billboards. In 1960, Historic Boston restored the building, and the Sandwich Time Shop on the left, and leased it to the Boston Globe that opened the Globe Corner Bookstore that anchored the corner for five decades.

Looking down Washington Street from Milk Street, the Old South Meetinghouse, once the tallest building in eighteenth-century Boston, is a prominent part of the streetscape. The large number of shops and restaurants include the Town Grill on the left, and on the right J. A. Tobacco and Cigar Shop, Berman's Radio Shop, a Howard Johnson's Restaurant, and an Arrow Shirt Shop.

The corner of Washington and School Streets was an Art Deco building that had Read All Bookstore, Henry's Cut Rate Jewelers, the School Street Camera Shop, which offered New England's largest selection of Kodak cameras and supplies. Notice the sign above the entrance to the camera shop stating "Peace of Mind Guaranteed!"

Raymond's was a well-known department store on Washington Street whose slogan was "Where U Bot The Hat." The store had the venerable Swamp Yankees Uncle Eph and Aunt Abby as their well-known spokespersons, which created one of the more outlandish and unique aspects of all the Boston stores. Raymond's also was quite adept at getting publicity, and with so much popular interest in Unkle Eph, Aunt Abby, and their village friends that in 1926 it was decided to have them visit the store in a steer-drawn turnbril cart and hold a gigantic sale while they were in town. This first Unkle Eph Day was such a wild success that it became a semi-annual event.

Jordan Marsh Department Store, seen on the right, was designed by Bradlee, Winslow & Wetherall and extended along Washington Street. In 1890, Jordan Marsh & Company claimed that "Our enormous business is felt in every commercial center, and the people of all nations are represented by their handiwork." *Continued on next page*

Right: In the early twentieth century, high-rise buildings were built along Washington Street, replacing the former three- and four-story Victorian blocks. With shops on the ground floor the upper floors had a variety of offices, dental and medical offices, as well as small businesses. Seen from the left are Hudson's, Wilson's, Lerner Shops, the Mary Jane Shop, and Gilchrist Department Store.

Below: The junction of Washington and Winter Streets had Albert's Hosiery Shop on the left and Gilchrist Department Store on the right. A large number of small shops lined Winter Street to Tremont Street, among them Topp's Restaurant on the left and Conrad and Chandler on the right.

Contined from previous page: By the turn of the twentieth century, it was not just the largest department store in New England but also offered unrivaled services to its shoppers and those who had store charges. With an unheard of money back guarantee if one was not pleased with their purchase, this policy in and of itself was to secure a loyal clientele who patronized the store.

Washington Street in July 1948 was almost deserted by shoppers with the summer heat. Seen from the left are Good Friend's and Murray Fur Shop, the Jewel Box, Summerfield's, with West Street, Yoland's American Girl Shoe Shop, Barbara Stone Coats and Dresses, Richard's Shop, S. S. Kresge's, Hudson's, and Gilchrist Department Store. With few automobiles, the traffic policeman on the far right seemingly had little to do.

Left: Looking north on Washington Street towards Avery Street, in 1948, shoppers walk along Washington Street, which was not only a leading shopping area but the entertainment district of the city. In the distance can be seen Liggett Rexall Drugstore, Clasby's, Karp's, Boyle's, the Paramount Theatre, RKO Keith's Theatre (later the Savoy Theatre and today the site is the Boston Opera House,) the Adams House, and the Modern Theatre (now a residence hall of Suffolk University.)

Opposite above: Washington Street curved as it reached Avery Street. On the right can be seen in the distance the State Theater, Howard Shoe Store, Pieronti's Restaurant, Prince Spaghetti House, Karp's, the Normandy Lounge, and the Paramount Theatre, which is showing in 1962 *Premature Burial*, a movie based upon the 1844 short story of the same name by Edgar Allan Poe and starring Ray Milland and Hazel Court. The movie was based in the nineteenth-century, and features a British aristocrat who is consumed with the fear of being buried alive. (*Courtesy of Kenneth McIntyre*)

Below: Two popular restaurants on Washington Street were Pieroni's Restaurant and Sea Grille, a restaurant begun in 1894 by the Pieroni Brothers who opened a chain of Pieroni's Sea Grilles, which proved immediately successful. The restaurant offered Bostonians foods such as Antipasto A L'Italienne, Seafood with a "secret seafood sauce," broiled lobster and prime rib of beef. On the right is the Prince Spaghetti House, which was to offer pasta and Italian food that was not well-known in Boston. Prince was founded in 1912 by Gaetano LaMarca, Giuseppe Seminara, and Michele Cantella, and by the 1950s, Joseph Pellegrino would open a chain of restaurants featuring Prince pasta and called this one Villa Prince. Who does not remember the slogan "Wednesday is Prince spaghetti day." This later became Crystal's Lounge and later The Haymarket, a gay club.

Joe and Nemo had a store in the Boylston Building, built in 1874, at the corner of Boylston and Washington Streets. Known as the "Hot Dog Kings," they had a chain of stores throughout the city. On the left is the King of Pizza, on the ground floor of the Boylston Building, designed by Carl Fehmer and built in 1887, and on the right Snyder's Army and Navy Store and the New Yorker Lounge. By the 1960s, the area was becoming increasingly tawdry and seedy after Scollay Square had been swept away by urban renewal.

The former Henry Siegal Department Store, at the corner of Washington and Essex Streets, had been repurposed in the 1920s with a theater and shops on the ground floor with offices above. The Essex Theatre replaced the former RKO Keith-Boston Theatre and the shops included Thom McAn Shoes, Mr. Alan's, and Canner's Furniture Store. The store was later converted to office space and is known as the Washington-Essex Building. On the far left is the State Theatre, which in 1973 was showing *Deep Throat* and *The Devil in Miss Jones*.

6

MOVIE PALACES ALONG WASHINGTON STREET

The RKO Keith-Boston was at the corner of Washington and Essex Streets in the former Seigel Department Store building, designed by Arthur Bowditch and built in 1905, that had been remodeled in the 1920s as an office building and stores and the theater on the ground floor. The marquee advertises the *Blind Date Show* with Arlene Francis and Bob Chester and his orchestra. This popular radio program, performed in front of a live audience, was a wildly popular show in the 1940s. (*Author's collection*)

Looking north on Washington Street from Kneeland Street the area was filled with movie palaces on both sides of the street in the early twentieth century. The Pastime Theatre, the Gaiety Theatre, the Park (State) Theatre, the Normnandie Theatre, Bijou Theatre, the Keith-Albee (RKO Boston Theatre,) Gordon's Olympia (Pilgrim) Theatre, the Globe (E. M. Loew's-Center) Theatre, and the Unique (Stuart) Theatre, and on the lower right the Washington Theatre and the Stuart Theatre were to bring Bostonians to this entertainment filled-block of Washington Street.

The Boston Music Hall was built in 1852 and was where the Boston Symphony performed until 1900 when they moved to Symphony Hall. The hall was converted for use as a vaudeville theater and operated under a number of different names including the Music Hall and the Empire Theatre. In 1906, it was renamed the Orpheum Theatre. In 1915, the theater was acquired by the Loew's Theaters. Loew's reopened the Orpheum in 1916 with a completely new interior designed by architect Thomas W. Lamb. The theater has hosted everything from vaudeville to symphony to movies and is now a rock concert venue. The Orpheum Theatre was host to a now-famous U2 concert and has hosted innumerable acts over the years. The marquee is advertising Lon Chaney and Roscoe "Fatty" Arbunkle who had often performed in vaudeville in the 1920s and 1930s.

RKO Keith's opened as the Keith-Albee Boston Theatre in 1925. The building had originally housed the Henry Siegel Department Store. The theater section was designed by Thomas W. Lamb as part the Keith-Albee-Orpheum chain of vaudeville theaters. Keith-Albee-Orpheum became part of RKO Pictures in 1928, and featured films, big band concerts, and variety theater performances. Musicians Benny Goodman, Tommy Dorsey, Glenn Miller, and others frequently played the theater. The marquee is advertising Ginger Rogers and Robert Ryan in *Tender Comrade*. On its right is the Modern Theatre and across the street the R. H. White Department Store.

The B. F. Keith Memorial Theatre was a vaudeville house that opened in 1928 with the film *Oh Kay*. This beautiful house later became part of the RKO theater chain and the RKO Keith's switched to a movies only format. The theater name was changed to the Savoy Theatre when it was purchased by Sack Theaters in 1965. Sold by Sack to the Opera Company of Boston, the theater became known as the Opera House, for which it was used until 1990. The theater was renovated, restored, and reopened in July 2004 by Clear Channel Entertainment, and is now a site for touring Broadway shows and other live entertainment. On the right is the Adams House Restaurant and Bar and the Mayflower Theatre.

The Paramount Theatre was designed by Arthur Bowditch and built in 1932 on Washington Street between Avery and West Streets. The theater was named for its original owner Paramount Pictures and was a 1,700-seat single-screen movie house that was one of the first theaters in Boston to show talking movies. Seen here in 1960, the marquee was advertising Alfred Hitchcock's movie *Psycho*, which is considered one of Hitchcock's best films and praised as a major work of cinematic art. Ranked among the greatest films of all time, it created acceptability for violence, deviant behavior and sexuality in American films and is widely considered to be the first of the slasher film genre. On the left was Sallinger's Department Store.

The RKO Keith-Boston was a popular theater and its neon marquee is advertising *Hollywood on Parade Revue* and *Seven Keys to Baldpate*, with a personal appearance by Gene Raymond in 1947. This was a farce with a famous author who arrives at Baldpate, a summer mountain resort in the dead of winter, determined to find peace and quiet to write his next book. But before his first night is out, a steady stream of unexpected visitors begins to fill the hotel—men and women with stories of love, loss, and flight, with none of them telling the truth.

7

The Combat Zone

Looking north on Washington Street from Kneeland Street, the area was a major entertainment district in the 1920s. In the distance can be seen the Gaiety Theatre, the State Theate, the Paramount Theatre, and the Globe Theatre. On the left is a sign advertising "Forverts," which is the Yiddish equivalent of *The Forward*, and the smaller type says "the biggest Yiddish daily newspaper in the world." Founded in 1897 as a Yiddish-language daily socialist newspaper, it launched an English-language weekly newspaper in 1990, and it is one of the most influential American Jewish publications. On the left is sign of the Sub Gum Restaurant and on the right are the marquees of the Globe (later E. M. Loew's, the Centre Theatre, and then the Pagoda and now Empire Garden) Washington and Stuart Theatres, and Jackson Furniture. (*Courtesy of John E. Lynes*)

Washington Street, for all of its historic and mercantile aspects, was to also include from the late 1950s to the 1990s the infamous Combat Zone, an area of the city that was on one hand dangerous and on the other titillating. Many of the adult businesses ousted from Scollay Square in the early 1960s moved to the nearby neighborhood already known as the Combat Zone. The name "Combat Zone" was popularized through a series of exposé articles on the area Jean Cole wrote for the *Boston Daily Record* in the 1960s. As this sign so poignantly states "You have nothing to fear except fear itself!"

The Liberty Tree Building was designed by J. H. Hammatt Billings and built at Washington and Essex Streets in 1850 on the site of the Liberty Tree Tavern and the Liberty Tree, which is seen in a third-floor bas relief. In 1900, Washburn Department Store, Pierson's Drug Store, and the Roman Catholic newspaper *The Pilot* occupied the building. By the 1960s, the ground floor of the building had the Essex Delicatessen (known for their delicious corned beef and hot pastrami sandwiches,) the Albiani Cafeteria, the Sherman Jewelry Shop, which was also a pawn shop, and on the second floor the Community Opticians Dentists and the Home of the Dickie-Blouse of Boston. The King of Pizza, run by Tony Pasquale, was in the Boylston Building on the right.

Dino's Pizza House was at the corner of Washington and Beach Streets, and was where patrons of the Combat Zone enjoyed two slices of pizza for a quarter. On the left can be seen Jerome's Bar and the Pilgrim Theatre. In a 1974 *Boston Herald* article, representatives of the Sack Theater Chain called the Combat Zone "Satan's playground" and "a malignancy comprised of pimps, prostitutes, erotica, and merchants of immorality" whose growth had to be curtailed before it spread throughout the city. The 5 acres of the Combat Zone was officially zoned for adult entertainment in 1974 to prevent the trend from spreading into other areas of the city.

As with Scollay Square during World War II, the Combat Zone also attracted servicemen on leave in Boston looking for a night on the town. Two sailors and two soldiers in uniform discuss which bar or club to go to as two young men on the left enter a cab. Nightlife in the Combat Zone was both exciting and alluring, especially for servicemen who had little shore leave for months at a time.

Upper: The Trans-Lux Theatre was originally known as Beethoven Hall and built in 1873. In the late nineteenth century, minstrel shows and variety shows were often featured on Washington Street just north of Boylston Street. By the late 1950s, the theater began showing adult films. Seen here they were showing *Thrill Girls of the Highway*, *The Violent Years*, and *The Desperate Women*, a trilogy that precluded that it was adults only who could enter the theater. Notice the Waldorf Restaurant on the right, part of a restaurant chain started in Boston in 1906.

Lower: The Trans-Lux later became the State Theatre and continued to show adult films. The marquee shows a double feature of *The Shocking Set*, where men were considered playthings, and *No Morals*, which had many men on the string. *The Shocking Set*, which was the first Boston showing, was advertised as "She had too much love for only one man." The premise of the movie was that three nudist roommates are unable to get their television to work, so they call a TV repairman to come and fix it. When the repairman gets there, he finds that not only is he having a hard time concentrating on fixing the set, but that all three of the girls are competing for his attention. Notice the Sandwich Fair shop on the right that also offered pizza, along with a bowling alley and pool tables.

A lobby with glass display cases at the State Theatre's "Newsreels" that could not fail to attract the attention of pedestrians with advertisements of the movies du jour. *The Skin Game* was "A Tale of Hot Cars, Cold Cash and Easy Women!" The first time shown in Boston, this movie said that they lived only for the excitement of each day and the pleasures of each night. The double feature also showed *The Wild Sex*, which was "More Daring Than Anything You've Ever Seen!"

The lobby of the State Theatre had a wonderful Art Deco stainless steel ticket booth with large poster display cases advertising the adult movie *du jour*. On the left is a life-sized cardboard cut out of a woman shivering in her polka dot bikini as it says "Welcome … It's so-o-o COOL inside." The movie poster on the right advertises the world premiere of *A Woman's Liberation*, an adult film on sex education, as well as *This is Hollywood*.

The marquee of the State Theatre was a bright spot on Washington Street in the evening and is seen advertising the first Boston showing of *Spiked Heels & Black Tights* and *The Depraved*. One Combat Zone patron quipped "Boston's old combat Zone evokes many a fond memory of a place when one could get lost in the seediness of the 'Red Light District.' Unlike the fictional television show bar *Cheers*, most of the bars along lower Washington Street were places where nobody wanted to know your name."

The Naked i on Washington Street is flanked by the Pilgrim Theatre on the left and the Liberty Books II that offered adult magazines and peep shows. *The Wall Street Journal* once called the Combat Zone of Boston "a sexual Disneyland" and the area was infamous for its erotic goddesses, strip clubs, peep shows, dirty bookstores, booze, drugs, and violence.

The bright lights of the Combat Zone in the 1970s was a magnet for Bostonians seeking excitement and diversion. The Pilgrim Theatre, which in the late 1960s began to offer old-fashioned burlesque, along with comedians (which was short lived), is seen in the 1980s offering three first run adult films, shown on a giant screen, and conveniently it was open all night. The Naked i, with its all seeing unblinking eye logo, offered a totally nude revue, which meant one had the option of a movie or a show, but whichever was the choice, neither would in any way disappoint.

These men, in matching groovy plaid polyester trousers, leave the Naked i after having watched the *Totally Nude College Girl Revue*. Some of the dancers' names from the Naked i were Suzanne, Kendra, Jasmine, Lynda, and Dori and the band was said to be terrific, but then, as with the other clubs, they were eventually replaced with a jukebox. Notice the employment sign on the right "Go Go Dancers and Bar Maids Wanted, Apply Within."

The Pilgrim Theatre was designed by Clarence Blackall as the Gordon's Olympia Theatre, owned by Nathan Gordon, and was later known as the Washington Street Olimpia, advertised as "The Theatre You Go To First." It was opened in 1912 showing photo plays and offering vaudeville acts. Here in the 1970s as the Pilgrim Theatre, the marquee advertises two new "stark realism" adult movies *Sexus* and *The Garden of Eden*, which were shown on a large cinema scope screen, one of the largest in Boston. The Archstone apartment building now stands on the former site of the Pilgrim Theatre.

A patron views the billboard of the adult movie that was now showing *She's Doing It Again*, an exposé of the *Way Out Set!* plus *Woman of Temptation*, which graphically showed the Raw Truth about the Girls of the Night. These were Exclusive First Boston Showing and why not see them, as the advertisement so poignantly states "Birds do it, Bees do it!" Of course, if one sought an alternative venue there was the Art Cinema on Tremont Street that offered the "finest X Rated all male movies."

An Art Deco stainless steel ticket booth in the Combat Zone was a remnant of when the theaters along Washington Street showed first run movies, and had elegant lobbies and appointments. Here the theater is showing in 1976 *Hot Nasties*, starring Susan Lynn Kiger in a unique erotic film with a plot, no less, to rival and expand anyone's wildest sexual fantasies.

Club 66 was a popular strip club that had neon signs of two 5-foot-tall dancing girls as a mirror image on either side of the sign above the tiled entrance. During the Combat Zone's heyday, some of the well-known strip clubs and lounges were the Naked i Cabaret, famous for its animated neon sign, which superimposed an all seeing eye over a woman's crotch; Club 66; the Teddy Bear Lounge; Show Bar; Good Time Charlie's; the Two O' Clock Lounge; Conway Men's Bar; Edward's Bar; the Glass Slipper; Piccadilly Bar; and Centerfolds.

Harry Sher, the "Boy from Dakota," advertised the Silver Dollar Bar as having "the finest fun and entertainment Boston offers." The bar that claimed it had the world's largest bar, had a logo of a silver dollar, minted in 1883, and which branded the popular bar that was actually a relatively peaceful place prior to the outbreak of war and the influx of servicemen, though it became a mecca for soldiers and sailors during World War II. The club offered four shows nightly in their Blue Terrace with notable headliners for its nightclub shows, and was one of the early gay friendly bars in the Combat Zone. Don Humbert wrote the song *Meet Me at the Silver Dollar*. A photographer could record your evening at the Silver Dollar, as seen here in 1943 with soldiers and their dates. (*Author's collection*)

The Silver Dollar Bar was one of the few bars in the Combat Zone that did not seem to have race or sexual discrimination, and like Izzy Ort's, it was a live music venue as well as a popular hangout for sailors and service men. Seen here in the 1940s, a sailor and his civilian friend pose at the bar with their pints of Seagram's 7. During World War II, there were said to be lots of rowdy sailors and lots of fights, fueled by cheap liquor and loud music day and night. But some of the music played at the Silver Dollar Bar was said to be pretty good, even if it was hard to hear it. The bar was sold in 1955 and became the Two O' Clock Lounge, which *Boston Magazine* said was "dark and dissolute and denizened with X-rated dancers."

The Pussy Cat Lounge was at the corner of Washington and Beach Streets, in a vivid blue painted facade with a white pussy cat with a curled tail as its logo. Advertising an all nude review, it drew its patrons like a bird to seed. Jessica Berson said that "Bostonians conjured a vision of the Zone as the center of the city's infectious vices, where the body was in constant danger of succumbing to its basest urges or falling victim to someone else's, where everything—sexuality, intimacy, identity—could be traded or exchanged."

The Mayflower Theatre was designed by Levi Newcomb as the Dobson Brothers Carpet Company store; it was remodeled by Clarence Blackall and opened in 1914 as a theater and was said to have the first sound projection equipment in the country as well as a double feature policy that spread throughout the industry. It was also one of the first movies-only deluxe theaters in New England. In 1949, its named was changed to Mayflower Theatre, which offered adult color films that were often the first run. Here the neon marquee advertises *Men in Action* and *Girls in 7-C*. Suffolk University created a new 185-seat multi-purpose Modern Theatre, with a restored facade, which opened in 2010.

Jazz musicians Sabby Lewis, Dick Wetmore, and Bullmoose Jackson regularly played at the Gilded Cage on Boylston Street. In 1960, the Gilded Cage tried a return to old-fashioned burlesque and hired Sally Keith, of Crawford House fame that had just been demolished in the West End Urban Renewal Project, to recreate her popular act and who by this time had been twirling her tassels for over twenty years. The bar was destroyed in 1966 when a leaking gas main exploded in the nearby Paramount Hotel, causing a five-alarm fire that killed eleven people.

The Scene XXX Adult Movies was a peep show with private viewing booths that conveniently offered "complete privacy" for patrons. For a quarter, patrons could view X-rated films that were said to be the "Tops in Adults Entertainment in Boston." Historically, a peep show was a form of entertainment provided by wandering showmen; however, they were now used for pornographic films or a live sex show, which is viewed through a viewing slot, which shuts after the time paid for has expired. Thus one has literally "peeped" at the show. On the left was the Intermission Lounge.

Jolar Cinema was at the corner of Essex and Washington Streets and had a neon sign that constantly flashed "Jolar Cinema Welcomes you to Boston's Entertainment Center." Jolar had twenty-three separate cubicles, each containing a coin-operated movie projector and six cubicles that accommodated two persons, and when the door was closed, a red light outside the cubicle turned on, warning others not to enter. For a quarter, one could view adult videos as attendants often yelled "Jolar, Jolar" to the patrons as they walked through the cinema. On the right is the E. M. Loew's Publix Theatre, formerly the Gayety, and the Book Mart. (*Courtesy of Bob Stone*)

Designed by noted architect H. H. Richardson as the Hayden Building, a Romanesque Revival commercial building built in 1875, used for commercial space with Lampson's Uniform Company with Sexton's Employment Service above in the 1940s. By the 1970s, the once-elegant building had the Scene XXX Adult Movies "Peep Arama" on the ground floor and the gay Club Baths above. In 1995, after a fire, Historic Boston Incorporated acquired the building and restored the exterior with the work done by the architectural firm Bruner/Cott and Preservation Carpentry students at the North Bennet Street School. In 2011, CUBE design and research converted the upper floors as condominiums with the ground floor as retail space. On the left is the Intermission Lounge.

Seen in a door way of a hotel in the Combat Zone, a drifter counts their money even though the sign offers rooms at moderate rates, which could be paid daily or weekly, the location of the hotel precluding a lack of comfort or quiet. Combat Zone patrons were besieged by "garish, grubby gauntlet[s] of sex-book stalls, theaters and 8-mm. peep shows for voyeurs" and they never failed to return for more. (*Courtesy of Elaine Croce*)

Chesty Morgan, whose real name was Liliana Wilczkowska, was a burlesque stripper who initially was known as the "Zsa Zsa Gabor of Burlesk." A nightclub owner suggested she call herself "Chesty Morgan," considering her voluminous 73-inch breasts. She never stripped below the waist, and in traditional burlesque fashion, valued the tease as much as the strip. Unlike many of the modern adult entertainment stars with large breasts, Morgan's were ironically not augmented with implants. According to the 1988 edition of *Guinness Movie Facts & Feats*, her bust measurement is the largest on record for a film star and in *Deadly Weapons*, "see the Mob get busted when 'Chesty' takes her revenge."

Tempest Storm, whose real name was Annie Blanche Banks, was called "The Queen Of Exotic Dancers." During her sixty-year career as a stripper, she was featured on the Pilgrim Theatre stage as "Tempest in a D cup," and in numerous men's magazines and burlesque movies, including *French Peep Show*, *Paris After Midnight*, *Striptease Girl*, *Teaserama*, and *Buxom Beautease*. Tempest Storm was inducted into the Burlesque Hall of Fame, where one of her oft used G-strings is now part of the museum's display.

Amber Mist, whose real name was Amber Levonch, was called in the 1960s the "Nation's No. 1 Ecdysiast," a more polite way to say striptease performer, and she tantalized the audiences at the Pilgrim Theatre, where she appeared along with fellow strippers Flame, Candy Stripe, and Silky Silvers. In 1965, the Pilgrim Theater began showing adult films and eventually it became Boston's last burlesque theater, alternating between the two forms of entertainment. When the Pilgrim Theatre closed in 1995, it was the last remaining X-rated movie house in Boston.

Satan's Angel, whose real name was Angel Cecelia Helene Walker, was billed as the "Devils own Mistress" and one of her popular acts was known as the "Ta Ta's Flambe," which was to light her tassels aflame, and then hopefully extinguish the flames by means of strenuous mammary rotation. She was known to be able to twirl five tassels at a time with two on her nipples, two on her buttocks, and one on her navel—what an artist! A trailblazer in her profession, she brought her talents to the Two O' Clock Lounge in the early 1970s.

Opposite below: Princess Cheyenne, dressed in an "Indian" headdresses with blue feathers and a beaded costume, was a headliner at the Naked i Cabaret on Washington Street in Boston. Few people realized that "royalty" danced in the Combat Zone, but the president of the *Harvard Lampoon* must have as he invited her to perform at a banquet in 1982, referring to her as "a nice and educated girl," she attended Emma Willard, which obviously condoned the striptease act as polite and acceptable in the Lampoon Castle, as she was stripping to work her way through college. One woman said that "when Princess Cheyenne came out on stage and danced ... to the song 'She's Got Betty Davis Eyes,' I knew that I wanted to reach her level of skill, if not status." The Naked i Cabaret, where Princess performed was a place where she "loved the dancing and the choreography. I loved the whole diva, temptress energy. That's such a great energy. The whole act of seduction is such a powerful thing."

Above: Fanne Foxe, whose real name was Annabelle Battistella, and was an exotic dancer known as "The Argentine Firecracker" and was well-received by patrons at the Pilgrim Theater in Boston. In fact, it was said that the crowd loved her performance. In September 1976, she was featured in *Playboy*, and again in February 1977. However, her stripteasing career literally took off once she began an affair with Wilbur Mills, and in 1975, she penned the book *The Stripper and the Congressman*.

Right: Wilbur Mills was a Congressman from Arkansas and was considered one of the most powerful members of the United States House of Representatives, and had once been a minor contender for the Democratic nomination for president in 1972. However, he often appeared at Fanne Foxe's shows at the Pilgrim Theatre and after the end of her act she told the audience "I'd like you to meet somebody," and she turned to the wings and called, "Mr. Mills, Mr. Mills! Where are you?" Mills strode onto the stage and during one of Foxe's introductions, he somehow managed to stumble off the stage into the orchestra pit. After exchanging a few words, she blew him a kiss, and after he got up he went back the way he came.

Wilbur Mills watches a feather-bedecked Fanne Foxe perform her act at the Pilgrim Theatre from a balcony box. During their affair, Mills and Foxe were in a car in Washington, which was pulled over by the police, and Foxe attempted to flee the scene by jumping into the Tidal Basin, after which she began referring to herself as "The Tidal Basin Bombshell." The incident attracted tremendous publicity, and eventually led to Mills' resignation two months later as chairman of the House Ways and Means Committee. He was re-elected to his congressional seat in 1974, but he did not run for re-election in 1976.

Jerome's Lounge was on Washington Street and would later be known as Jerome's Naked i and then just plain old Naked i. Jerome's would advertise their sorority strippers as a "Totally Nude College Girl Review," which certainly caught the attention of Bostonians. Roswell Angier took this photograph in 1975 of three bar patrons intently staring at the stripper, obviously between college classes, with incredulous looks on their faces. As Mark Feeney said in the *Boston Globe*: "There's no real in between in the Zone, little or no sense of human connection. That's as it should be." There was literally something for everyone in the Combat Zone, and it really was not always a bad thing. (*Collection Boston Museum of Fine Arts*)

Right: Playland Cafe was opened on Essex Street by Rocco Staffier in 1937 as a cafe and bar, and by the start of World War II, it had begun attracting a gay clientele. Considered the oldest gay bar in Boston, the crowd at Playland was surprisingly diverse for its time, both racially and in terms of class. Neil Miller recounted that "Blue-collar truck drivers mingled with Harvard students." In 2007, *Boston Globe* reporter Robert Sullivan recalled Playland as "a Combat Zone bar known for its sketchy clientele, banged-up piano, and year-round Christmas lights." It truly was a memorable bar and never to be forgotten.

Below: Izzy Ort's Golden Nugget, on the left, was a hopping place in the 1940s. Many well-known musicians played on two floors, among them Murray Onigman and his nineteen-piece big band "The Bob Murray Orchestra," he sang lead on one of the earliest recordings in 1944 of the Bobby Troup Song "Route 66." In the main room at street level, and in a room upstairs called El Tropico, patrons had dancing to many jazz performers among them Sam Rivers, Ruby Braff, Herb Pomeroy, and Quincy Jones. Izzy Ort's was one of the first strip bars in what would later become known as Boston's Combat Zone. As a popular hangout for rowdy sailors, it was notorious among musicians for being a rough place to play.

Looking south on Washington Street in the 1970s with its colorful neon lights and marquees, the Combat Zone had the State Theater on the right, which offered first run adult movies and was open all night, the State II, the Publix, Jolar Cinema, the Paramount Theatre, Naked i with the high-rise buildings of the New England Medical Center overshadowing the area. The *Boston Globe* began referring to certain theaters in the Combat Zone as "notorious gathering places for homosexuals" and unseemly activity was reported as taking place in the once popular theaters.

According to Jessica Berson: "The downfall of the Combat Zone was real estate, not murder. In the emerging economic boom, the City suddenly realized that some of its most valuable land was occupied by its least valued citizens. For the second time in thirty years, Boston demolished its adult entertainment district. Luxury condominium towers rose from the rubble, but Bostonians retain the memory of the erotic possibilities the Zone extended to performers and customers alike." Washington Street had Jolar Cinema, Boston Bunnies, Live Nudes, Peep Shows and Rap Booths, the Pilgrim Theater, the Show Bar, and the Naked i.